Star Gazing...

Welcome to my new book. Before we look up at the sky, I wanted to say hi and introduce myself. I'm Jake, and I write books. Some folks might call it a job, but to me it feels more like a mix of school, playtime, work, and wild discovery—all rolled into one. I spend my days reading, researching, writing, and wondering about the world (and the universe!) around us. Sure, it gets tricky sometimes, but honestly? I wouldn't trade it for anything.

Lately, I've been diving deep into the most extreme stuff I can find—volcanoes, tornadoes, earthquakes… the wild, unstoppable forces of nature right here on Earth. And also, extreme animals—sharks, snakes, spiders and so on. But the more I wrote about our planet, the more I started looking *up*. Into space. Into the unknown. That's when I got hooked on black holes. They're not just powerful—they're mysterious, mind-bending, and still full of secrets. This book is your invitation to explore them with me.

When you look up into the sky at night and see the stars shining back at you, you are effectively looking back in time. These stars are so far away, that it takes years — thousands, sometimes millions — of years for the light to reach us on earth. Some of those stars have died long before the light even reaches us and we can see them. In some ways, we are time-travelling just by looking at a star that isn't there any more. This poses a lot more questions than it answers, doesn't it!?

So here's a big question. What happens when a star dies?

Imagine a star—bigger than our sun—burning bright for millions of years. Then... it runs out of fuel. It collapses in on itself, crushing everything into a point so small, so dense, that not even light can escape it.

That's a black hole.

Sound like science fiction? It's not. Black holes are real—and they're some of the weirdest, most powerful things in the entire universe.

In this book, we're going to explore the truth behind these cosmic monsters. You'll find out:

- What a black hole actually *is* (and why it's not a giant vacuum cleaner)

- How they form, where to find them, and what would happen if you got too close

- What happens to time, space, and matter near a black hole

- And the wild theories scientists are still debating, like wormholes and alternate realities

You don't need a spaceship or a PhD to get started—just curiosity. If you've ever looked up at the night sky and wondered what's out there you're in the right place. To understand more about black holes, you're just going to need to open up your mind, flick the switch called 'imagination' and be ready to delve into ideas that are sometimes more far-fetched than most of the boring real stuff we live with on Planet Earth. Space is whacky, weird and wonderful.

One of the best ways to learn is to hear or read something more than once—so I do that *on purpose* in my books. If you catch yourself thinking, "Hey Jake, you already told me that!"—that's a *great* sign. It means the information is really starting to stick.

Oh, and one more thing: there's a meaty, mighty quiz waiting for you at the end—with easy, medium, and hard questions. So stay sharp… you might just end up teaching *your teacher* a thing or two.

Ready to dive into the most mysterious places in space?

By the way: If you love this book, check out my books in the *Extreme Animals* series (sharks, big cats, spiders, snakes…), and also my *Extreme Earth* series too — about hurricanes, tornadoes, volcanoes, wildfires and more! I would love to know what you'd be interested in reading about—so if you want you can send an email (that I promise to read)… you can send it through my publisher:

support@blendonpublishing.com

You could write and tell me what facts you found most fascinating, or whether I told you something you didn't know before. Even if you just want to write and tell me how you think this book could have been even better, that's fine too! I'd love to hear your thoughts, and it's so cool to know who's reading.

I'm not an expert on black holes…I'm not an expert on anything really, except maybe choosing cool things to write books about. I'm just a writer who finds lots of different things fascinating and I love to learn. I'm not a teacher…I'm right here, learning with you.

Finally: just after the last chapter, I am going to provide a link so that you—or whoever bought you this book—can hopefully go on Amazon and leave it a review and star rating. This really helps me reach more readers your age who might like my writing. I would be SO grateful if you would do that for me.

Enjoy!

Jake :)

🚀 Before You Blast Off: Some "Must-Know" Words

Before we zoom into black holes, it helps to get comfy with some space lingo you'll see again and again. These aren't just big science words—they're your launchpad to understanding the universe. There's a full 'glossary' at the end of the book too.

Event Horizon
The invisible "point of no return" around a black hole. Once something crosses this line, it's gone for good. No escape. Not even for light.

Singularity
The mysterious core of a black hole where everything gets squished into a super-dense point. It's the part that blows scientists' minds—and we still don't fully understand it.

Accretion Disk
A hot, glowing, spinning ring of gas and dust that circles some black holes like a whirlpool. It's what we *can* see, and it helps scientists find black holes.

Gravitational Waves
Ripples in space and time caused by huge cosmic events—like black holes crashing into each other.

Scientists can now *detect* these waves, which is pretty awesome.

Supermassive Black Hole
A ginormous black hole (millions or billions of times heavier than our sun) found in the center of most galaxies—including our own!

Wormhole
A theoretical shortcut through space and time. Some scientists think black holes *might* connect to them. No one's found one yet... but it makes for epic sci-fi.

Time Dilation
Time slows down near massive objects like black holes. If you hung out near one (not recommended!), time would move differently for you than for people on Earth.

Hawking Radiation
An idea from scientist Stephen Hawking: black holes might *slowly* lose energy and shrink over time. Yep—even black holes might fade away eventually.

Spaghettification
Sounds funny, but it's real science! It's what happens when gravity stretches an object as it falls into a black hole—like stretching spaghetti. Yikes.

1: What is a Black Hole?

The Basics of Black Holes

Black holes are one of the most fascinating objects in space. They are regions where gravity is so strong that nothing, not even light, can escape from them. Imagine a giant vacuum cleaner in the universe, sucking up everything around it! While we can't see black holes directly, scientists know they exist because of the way they affect nearby stars and gas. They can be found in various sizes, but the biggest ones are called supermassive black holes, often located at the centers of galaxies.

The formation of black holes is an exciting process that starts with massive stars. When these stars run out of fuel, they can no longer support themselves against gravity. This leads to a dramatic collapse, and if the star is big enough, it can create a black hole. There are also smaller black holes known as stellar black holes, which form from smaller stars. Understanding how black holes form helps scientists learn more about the life cycle of stars and the evolution of our universe.

In popular culture, black holes have become a favorite subject in movies, books, and video games. They are often depicted as mysterious gateways to other dimensions or as the ultimate villains in a space adventure. Movies like Interstellar showcase the strange effects of black holes, including how they can warp time and space. This creative portrayal captures the imagination of many, making black holes not just scientific phenomena but also a source of entertainment.

Scientists also study black holes to understand their role in the universe. Supermassive black holes can have a significant impact on their galaxies, influencing the formation of stars and the movement of galaxies themselves. Additionally, black holes are linked to gravitational waves, which are ripples in space-time caused by massive objects moving.

By observing these waves, scientists can learn more about the properties of black holes and the universe's expansion.

The mystery of black holes also opens the door to exciting theories about time travel. Some scientists speculate that black holes might act as gateways to other parts of the universe or even different times. While these ideas sound like they belong in a science fiction story, they are based on real scientific principles.

As research continues, who knows what secrets black holes may reveal about time and space in the future?

How Are Black Holes Formed?

Black holes are some of the most mysterious objects in the universe, and their formation is a fascinating process. Most black holes start as massive stars. When these stars exhaust their nuclear fuel, they can no longer support themselves against gravity. This leads to a dramatic collapse, resulting in a supernova explosion that blasts away the outer layers of the star, leaving behind a dense core.

If the core is heavy enough, it continues to collapse under its own weight, creating a black hole. This point of no return is known as the event horizon. Once something crosses this boundary, it cannot escape the black hole's powerful gravitational pull.

This makes black holes invisible, as they don't emit light, but they can be detected by observing their effects on nearby stars and gas.

There are different types of black holes, including stellar black holes, which form from individual stars, and supermassive black holes, which can be millions or even billions of times more massive than the Sun. These supermassive black holes are usually found at the center of galaxies, including our own Milky Way.

Scientists believe they formed from the merging of smaller black holes and the accumulation of gas and stars over billions of years.

Black holes are not just fascinating cosmic objects; they also play a significant role in our understanding of the universe. They affect the motion of stars and galaxies around them and can even influence the formation of new stars. Moreover, when two black holes collide, they create ripples in spacetime known as gravitational waves, which scientists can detect here on Earth.

In popular culture, black holes capture the imagination of many through movies, books, and games, often associated with time travel and adventure. While the reality of black holes is rooted in complex science, their portrayal in stories sparks curiosity and encourages young minds to explore the wonders of the universe.

Understanding how black holes form helps us grasp their importance in the cosmic story, making them not just mysterious but also vital components of our galaxy.

Types of Black Holes

When we think about black holes, we often imagine something mysterious and powerful in space. There are actually different types of black holes, each with unique characteristics. The three main types are stellar black holes, supermassive black holes, and intermediate black holes. Stellar black holes are formed when massive stars collapse at the end of their life cycle, creating a gravitational pull so strong that nothing can escape it.

Supermassive black holes are the giants of the black hole family. They can be millions to billions of times heavier than our sun. These black holes are usually found at the centers of galaxies, including our own Milky Way.

Scientists believe that supermassive black holes help shape galaxies and influence the stars and gas around them. They are fascinating because they raise many questions about how they formed and evolved over time.

Intermediate black holes are a bit of a mystery. They are larger than stellar black holes but smaller than supermassive ones, weighing between hundreds to thousands of solar masses. Scientists think they might form when smaller black holes merge, but we still don't have enough evidence to fully understand them.

Discovering more about intermediate black holes could help us learn more about the universe's history.

Black holes have also made their way into popular culture, appearing in movies, books, and games. These portrayals often spark curiosity about what black holes really are. While movies might exaggerate their power, they help introduce the concept of black holes to young audiences.

Understanding black holes can lead to exciting discussions about physics, space travel, and even time travel theories.

Finally, black holes play a crucial role in cosmology, the study of the universe's origin and evolution. They are connected to gravitational waves, which are ripples in space-time caused by massive cosmic events. By studying these waves, scientists can learn more about black holes and the universe itself. The more we explore these cosmic giants, the more we discover about the fundamental laws of nature and our place in the universe.

Fascinating Fact

Black holes don't actually "suck" things in—they pull objects with gravity, just like Earth does. They just happen to have *really* strong gravity.

Chapter 1 – Key Takeaways

- A black hole forms when a massive star collapses under its own gravity.

- Black holes have incredibly strong gravity that nothing—not even light—can escape.

- The idea of a black hole started as a theory before scientists found real evidence.

- Black holes challenge our understanding of space, time, and the laws of physics.

2: Theoretical Models of Black Holes

Understanding the Science Behind Black Holes

Black holes are one of the most fascinating and mysterious objects in space. They form when massive stars collapse under their own gravity, creating a point of no return known as the event horizon. Once something crosses this boundary, it cannot escape the immense gravitational pull of the black hole.

This is what makes black holes so intriguing to scientists and curious minds alike, especially for young explorers eager to understand the universe's secrets.

Theoretical models help astronomers understand how black holes behave and interact with their surroundings. These models suggest that black holes can vary in size, with some being just a few times the mass of our Sun, while others, known as supermassive black holes, can be millions or even billions of times heavier.

Supermassive black holes are often found at the centers of galaxies, including our own Milky Way, where they play a crucial role in the formation and evolution of galaxies.

Black holes have also captured the imagination of people in popular culture. They appear in movies, books, and video games, often portrayed as mysterious gateways to other dimensions or as powerful forces that can consume everything in their path. This fascination helps spark interest in science and encourages young people to learn more about astrophysics and the wonders of the universe.

Recent discoveries in astrophysics have shown that black holes can create gravitational waves, ripples in space-time caused by massive objects in motion. When two black holes collide, they send out these waves, which can be detected by specialized instruments on Earth. This groundbreaking research offers a new way to study black holes and understand their properties, providing thrilling insights into their role in the cosmos.

The idea of black holes also connects to exciting theories about time travel. Some scientists speculate that if we could navigate near a black hole, it might be possible to experience time differently, leading to the concept of time travel.

While this idea remains in the realm of theory—meaning it is not really proven, it is what scientists think is the truth—it sparks the imagination of many young minds, encouraging them to think critically about time, space, and the mysteries of the universe.

The Event Horizon Explained

The event horizon is one of the most fascinating aspects of black holes. Imagine a point in space where gravity is so strong that nothing, not even light, can escape. This boundary is what we call the event horizon. Once something crosses this line, it is lost to the universe forever. It's like a one-way door that leads to a mysterious place where the rules of physics as we know them don't apply anymore.

When scientists talk about black holes, they often refer to the event horizon as the "point of no return." This is because anything that gets too close risks being pulled in by the black hole's immense gravitational force. It's important to note that the event horizon isn't a physical surface we can touch or see. Instead, it's an invisible area that marks the limits of the black hole's influence. Just beyond this boundary, the forces of nature act differently than they do in everyday life.

In popular culture, black holes and their event horizons have captured the imagination of many. Movies, books, and video games often depict them as swirling vortexes that can transport characters to different dimensions or times.

While these stories are fun and exciting, they are often far from the reality of what black holes are like. The truth is, they are much more mysterious and complex than any adventure tale can suggest.

Black holes, especially the supermassive ones found at the centers of galaxies, play a crucial role in our understanding of the universe. They can help scientists learn about the formation and evolution of galaxies. By studying the light and other radiation emitted from the area around the event horizon, researchers can gather clues about the black hole and its effects on surrounding stars and gas.

This research can even lead to exciting discoveries about gravitational waves, which are ripples in spacetime caused by massive objects like black holes.

Lastly, the concept of time travel is often linked to black holes and their event horizons. Some scientists theorize that if we could somehow survive crossing the event horizon, we might find ourselves in a different time or place in the universe.

Although this idea is still also purely theoretical, it shows just how intriguing black holes can be. They are not just cosmic vacuum cleaners, but gateways to understanding time, space, and the mysteries of our galaxy.

Singularity: What Lies at the Center?

At the heart of every black hole lies a mysterious region called the singularity. This is where the laws of physics as we know them seem to disappear. Imagine a point in space where gravity pulls so strongly that nothing, not even light, can escape. It's a place where time and space are twisted into an incredible knot, creating a puzzle that scientists are still trying to unravel. The singularity is often described as a point of infinite density, where all the matter that once made up the black hole is concentrated.

Many scientists believe that understanding singularities could help unlock the secrets of the universe. Theoretical models suggest that these regions could hold clues about the very nature of space and time. Some even theorize that singularities could be gateways to other dimensions or parallel universes! This idea captures the imagination and inspires stories in books and movies, where characters might travel through black holes to other worlds.

In popular culture, black holes and their singularities have sparked the creativity of filmmakers and writers. Movies like Interstellar dive deep into the concept of black holes, showcasing stunning visuals and exciting adventures.

These stories often highlight how black holes can bend time, allowing characters to experience time differently. This concept of time travel, linked to the singularity, makes black holes not just a topic of science, but also a fascinating element of storytelling.

Scientists are also studying how black holes affect their surroundings. Supermassive black holes at the centers of galaxies can influence star formation and the movement of stars. The powerful gravitational pull from a black hole can create a dynamic environment, where gas and dust swirl around at incredible speeds. This interaction generates gravitational waves, ripples in space-time that are now being detected by advanced instruments on Earth. Observing these waves helps astronomers learn more about the universe and the role of black holes within it.

In conclusion, the singularity at the center of black holes remains one of the greatest mysteries in astronomy. As we continue to explore the cosmos, scientists hope to unlock the secrets held within these enigmatic regions. The journey to understand singularities not only pushes the boundaries of science but also fuels our imagination, reminding us of the wonders that lie in the universe. Who knows what we might discover next?

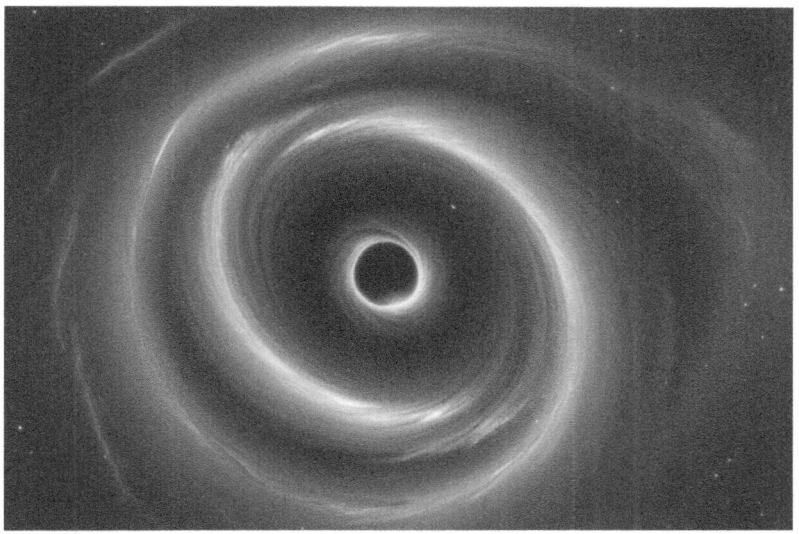

Fascinating Fact

The supermassive black hole at the center of our galaxy is called Sagittarius A*, and it's about four million times the mass of our Sun!

Chapter 2 – Key Takeaways

- There are three main types of black holes: stellar, intermediate, and supermassive.

- Stellar black holes are the smallest, formed from collapsing stars.

- Supermassive black holes live at the center of galaxies and are millions of times heavier than the Sun.

- Intermediate black holes are hard to find but may exist in star clusters or dwarf galaxies.

3: Supermassive Black Holes in Galaxies

What Makes a Black Hole Supermassive?

Supermassive black holes are among the most mysterious objects in the universe. They are found at the centers of galaxies and can be millions or even billions of times the mass of our sun. But what makes them supermassive? Scientists believe that their formation begins with smaller black holes merging together over time, drawing in gas and stars from their surroundings. This process allows them to grow larger and larger, accumulating an enormous amount of mass.

One key factor in the growth of supermassive black holes is the matter they consume. As they pull in gas and dust from nearby stars, they create a swirling disk of material around them. This disk heats up and emits light, allowing astronomers to detect the presence of a black hole even though it cannot be seen directly. The more matter a black hole consumes, the bigger it becomes, leading to their supermassive classification.

The environment around supermassive black holes also plays a crucial role in their development. Galaxies are constantly interacting and merging, which can funnel more material into the black hole.

These interactions can lead to bursts of star formation and even trigger the black hole's growth as it devours more stars and gas. This dynamic process is what makes galaxies exciting and ever-changing places in the universe.

In popular culture, supermassive black holes have captured the imagination of many, appearing in movies and books as mysterious and powerful entities. They are often portrayed as cosmic monsters that can bend time and space. This fascination helps spark curiosity about real-life black holes and the scientific theories that surround them, inspiring future scientists and explorers to learn more about our universe.

Finally, supermassive black holes are not just fascinating objects; they also play a significant role in shaping the cosmos. They influence the formation and evolution of galaxies, and their gravitational pull can affect the movement of stars and gas in their vicinity. By studying these giant black holes, scientists can gain insights into the history of the universe and the forces that govern its structure. The mysteries of supermassive black holes continue to be a frontier of scientific exploration, inviting young minds to ponder the wonders of space.

The Role of Supermassive Black Holes in Galaxies

Supermassive black holes are some of the most fascinating objects in the universe, and they play a crucial role in the formation and evolution of galaxies. These colossal entities, often found at the centers of galaxies, can have masses that are millions to billions of times that of our Sun. Their immense gravitational pull influences the motion of stars and gas surrounding them, shaping the structure of galaxies and the way they evolve over time.

When a galaxy forms, it begins with clouds of gas and dust coming together under gravity. As the galaxy grows, supermassive black holes can form from the collapse of massive stars or through the merging of smaller black holes. This process helps to create a powerful gravitational center, which can attract more matter and contribute to the galaxy's growth. The presence of a supermassive black hole can also affect how stars are born and how they move within the galaxy.

Supermassive black holes are not just empty voids; they are surrounded by an accretion disk made up of gas and dust that spirals into them. As matter falls into the black hole, it heats up and emits energy in the form of light and X-rays.

This phenomenon can outshine entire galaxies, making supermassive black holes some of the brightest objects in the universe. Scientists study these emissions to learn more about the black holes themselves and the galaxies they inhabit.

Additionally, supermassive black holes play a significant role in the dynamics of galaxies. They can create powerful jets that shoot out into space, influencing the surrounding environment. These jets can impact star formation and even contribute to the heating of gas in the galaxy, preventing it from collapsing to form new stars. Thus, supermassive black holes are not just passive entities but active participants in the cosmic dance of galaxy formation.

In popular culture, supermassive black holes often capture the imagination of writers and filmmakers, representing the ultimate mystery of the universe. They spark our curiosity about space, time, and the unknown. As scientists continue to uncover the secrets of these gigantic black holes, they reveal more about the history of our universe and our place within it. Understanding the role of supermassive black holes in galaxies helps us appreciate the complex and dynamic cosmos we live in.

Famous Supermassive Black Holes

When we look up at the night sky, we see millions of stars twinkling away. But did you know that some of those stars are hiding something incredible behind them? Supermassive black holes, which are millions or even billions of times heavier than our sun, are found at the centers of most galaxies! These mysterious giants can be difficult to spot, but scientists have found ways to study them and understand their immense power.

One of the most famous supermassive black holes is called Sagittarius A*, located at the center of our Milky Way galaxy. It's so massive that it has a gravitational pull strong enough to keep stars and other objects in orbit around it. When scientists discovered it, they realized they were looking at a giant that had shaped our galaxy for billions of years. Learning about Sagittarius A* helps us understand not just our galaxy, but also the universe itself!

Another well-known supermassive black hole is M87*. This black hole is located in the Virgo galaxy cluster and is famous for being the first black hole ever photographed! In 2019, scientists used a network of telescopes around the world to capture an image of its shadow, proving that black holes are real and allowing us to see something that was once only imagined in science fiction.

This event excited many people and sparked interest in black holes across the globe.

Supermassive black holes are not just fascinating because of their size and power; they also play a crucial role in the life cycle of galaxies. They can influence star formation and even help galaxies grow. Some scientists believe that supermassive black holes could be linked to gravitational waves, ripples in space-time caused by massive events like black hole collisions. Understanding these connections helps us learn more about how the universe works.

In popular culture, black holes often appear in movies and books, capturing the imagination of audiences everywhere. These stories sometimes explore themes of time travel and the mysteries of the universe.

While they may be fictional, they inspire curiosity and creativity, encouraging young minds to explore the science behind these cosmic wonders.

So, the next time you gaze up at the stars, remember that there are supermassive black holes out there, shaping our universe in ways we are just beginning to understand!

Fascinating Fact

If you fell into a black hole feet first, your feet would feel much more gravity than your head—this is why scientists call the stretching effect "spaghettification."

Chapter 3 – Key Takeaways

- Black holes have extreme gravity that can bend light and stretch objects.

- Time slows down near a black hole—a phenomenon known as time dilation.

- Falling into a black hole would stretch you into spaghetti (spaghettification!).

- The event horizon is the invisible boundary— once crossed, there's no return.

4: Black Holes and Gravitational Waves

What Are Gravitational Waves?

Gravitational waves are like ripples in a pond, but instead of water, they travel through the fabric of space and time. These waves are created when massive objects, like black holes or neutron stars, collide or move rapidly. Imagine two black holes spinning around each other and then crashing together; this event sends out waves that can travel across the universe! Scientists believe that detecting these waves can help us learn more about the universe and the mysterious objects within it.

In 2015, scientists made a groundbreaking discovery when they detected gravitational waves for the first time. This was a huge moment in the world of astronomy, as it opened up a new way to observe the cosmos. The waves were caused by two black holes merging, and this event occurred about 1.3 billion years ago. By catching these waves, scientists were able to learn about the properties of black holes and how they behave, which had only been theorized before.

Gravitational waves are important because they allow us to see things that traditional telescopes cannot. While regular telescopes capture light and images from distant stars and galaxies, gravitational waves give us a different perspective. They provide information about the movement and interactions of massive objects, revealing secrets about the universe's history and evolution.

In popular culture, black holes and gravitational waves have captured the imagination of many. Movies and books often depict black holes as mysterious gateways to other dimensions or time travel.

With the real discovery of gravitational waves, scientists are now able to explore these concepts in more depth, turning some of the wild ideas from science fiction into potential reality.

As we continue to study gravitational waves, we unlock new mysteries about supermassive black holes and their role in galaxies. Each wave detected adds another piece to the puzzle of understanding how our universe works. Who knows what other secrets these cosmic ripples might reveal about time, space, and the very structure of reality?

How Black Holes Create Gravitational Waves

Black holes are some of the most fascinating objects in the universe, and they have a special ability to create something called gravitational waves. These waves are ripples in space and time, much like the ripples you see when you throw a stone into a pond.

When two black holes collide or orbit each other, they create these waves, which can travel across the universe and reach our planet. Scientists have developed ways to detect these tiny waves, helping us learn more about black holes and their mysterious behaviors.

Imagine two supermassive black holes, each millions of times heavier than our Sun, spiraling around each other in the center of a distant galaxy. As they get closer, they move faster and faster, causing their gravitational pull to grow stronger. When they finally collide, it creates a huge burst of energy and sends out gravitational waves that can be felt even billions of light-years away. This is a cosmic event that can help us understand how black holes grow and how they shape the galaxies around them.

Gravitational waves were first predicted by Albert Einstein over a hundred years ago, but it wasn't until recently that we could actually detect them. In 2015, scientists at the LIGO (Laser Interferometer Gravitational-Wave Observatory) observatory made history by capturing the sound of two black holes merging. This discovery opened up a new way of observing the universe, allowing us to hear the universe's most dramatic events. It's like listening to the universe sing its own song!

In popular culture, black holes often appear as mysterious portals or gateways to other dimensions. While some stories are purely fictional, scientists are exploring the real-life implications of black holes on our understanding of time and space. The gravitational waves created by these cosmic giants offer clues about how time behaves near a black hole, leading to exciting theories about time travel and what might lie beyond our current understanding of the universe.

As we continue to study black holes and their gravitational waves, we are uncovering more about the universe's secrets. Each discovery helps us piece together the puzzle of how galaxies form and evolve over time.

The study of black holes is not just about understanding these fascinating objects; it's about understanding our place in the cosmos and the nature of reality itself. Who knows what amazing things we will discover next?

Detecting Gravitational Waves

Gravitational waves are ripples in space-time caused by massive objects, like black holes, colliding in the universe. When two black holes orbit each other and eventually merge, they create powerful waves that travel through space. These waves are incredibly weak by the time they reach Earth, but scientists have developed special instruments to detect them. It's like trying to feel a tiny pebble dropped in a vast ocean, but these instruments are super sensitive and can pick up the smallest changes.

The first direct detection of gravitational waves happened in 2015, a monumental event in the world of astronomy. Scientists at the LIGO facility found the waves created by two black holes merging about 1.3 billion light-years away! This discovery confirmed the prediction made by Albert Einstein over a century ago, showing that gravitational waves are not just a theory but a reality of our universe.

Detecting gravitational waves has opened a new window into the study of black holes and the mysteries of the cosmos. Before this, black holes were mostly studied through their effects on nearby stars and gas. Now, with gravitational waves, astronomers can observe black holes in a completely new way, leading to exciting discoveries about their formation and behavior.

In popular culture, black holes have often been depicted as swirling maelstroms or doorways to other dimensions. However, the science behind them is even more fascinating. Understanding gravitational waves helps us piece together the puzzles of the universe, including how galaxies evolve and how time might behave near these colossal objects. It's as if we've been given a new set of tools to explore the universe.

As we continue to improve our technology and understanding of gravitational waves, who knows what mysteries we might uncover? The universe is full of wonders, and black holes are among its greatest secrets.

By learning about these waves, young explorers like you can be part of the exciting journey of discovery, helping scientists understand the very fabric of our universe and the role black holes play in it.

Fascinating Fact:

The first real picture of a black hole was taken in 2019. It showed a glowing ring of gas around the black hole in a galaxy called M87.

Chapter 4 – Key Takeaways

- Black holes are invisible but can be detected by how they affect nearby stars and gas.

- Accretion disks are glowing rings of material spinning around black holes.

- Some black holes shoot powerful jets of energy into space.

- Black holes can cause stars to wobble, disappear, or orbit strangely.

5: Black Holes in Popular Culture

Black Holes in Movies and TV Shows

Black holes have captured the imagination of filmmakers and television creators for decades. These mysterious cosmic objects, which pull everything into their grasp, often serve as a backdrop for thrilling adventures in popular culture.

In movies like "Interstellar," black holes are portrayed with stunning visuals, showcasing their swirling disks of gas and the possibility of time travel. This sparks curiosity and leads many young viewers to wonder about the real science behind these fascinating phenomena.

Television shows also explore the concept of black holes in creative ways. For instance, in series like "Doctor Who," black holes are not just scientific mysteries but gateways to different dimensions and times. These stories allow kids to dream about traveling through space and encountering incredible worlds, all while introducing them to complex theories in an entertaining format. The blend of science fiction with real science helps demystify black holes, making them accessible to a younger audience.

In addition to entertainment, black holes play a significant role in our understanding of the universe. They are often depicted as the ultimate end point for massive stars, leading to discussions about their formation and the effects of their immense gravity.

Documentaries and educational programs delve into how black holes can warp space and time, presenting an exciting way for kids to learn about concepts like gravitational waves. This connection between science and popular culture can ignite a passion for astrophysics in the next generation.

Many stories also incorporate the idea of supermassive black holes, which are found at the centers of galaxies. Films and shows sometimes illustrate the idea that these giant black holes can influence the formation of stars and planets. This depiction not only entertains but also educates children about the structure of our galaxy and the universe at large. By making these concepts relatable, young audiences can develop a deeper appreciation for the cosmos.

As children engage with black holes through movies and television, they are encouraged to ask questions and seek answers. This curiosity leads to further exploration of scientific ideas, such as the possibility of time travel and the mysteries of dark matter.

By bridging the gap between entertainment and education, black holes in popular culture serve as a springboard for young minds to explore the wonders of the universe, inspiring future scientists and dreamers alike.

Books and Comics Featuring Black Holes

Books and comics often serve as windows into the fascinating world of black holes, captivating the imaginations of young readers. One popular series, "The Black Hole Chronicles," takes its audience on thrilling adventures through space, where characters encounter supermassive black holes and learn about their mysterious properties. These stories blend science with fiction, allowing children to explore complex concepts in a fun and engaging way. Each book introduces new theoretical models of black holes, making it easier for readers to grasp the incredible phenomena surrounding these cosmic giants.

In addition to novels, comics have made a significant impact in portraying black holes. Titles like "Galactic Adventures: Black Hole Quest" feature colorful illustrations and action-packed plots that draw children into the science behind black holes. The characters often face challenges posed by gravitational waves, showcasing how these waves are linked to the presence of black holes in our universe. Through humor and adventure, these comics explain the role of black holes in cosmology and how they affect the fabric of space-time.

Many of these stories also delve into the idea of time travel, a concept closely associated with black holes. In "Time Warp: Journey through a Black Hole," young explorers find themselves navigating through different time periods after being sucked into a black hole. This imaginative twist not only entertains but also encourages readers to ponder the theories of time travel that scientists have proposed. Such narratives inspire curiosity about the universe and the scientific principles that govern it.

Furthermore, these books and comics often feature real scientific discoveries alongside fictional tales. Authors consult astrophysicists to ensure that the information presented is accurate and up-to-date. This blend of fact and fiction helps children understand that while black holes are fascinating and often portrayed in fantastical ways, they are real phenomena studied by scientists. By presenting black holes in various contexts, these narratives make learning about space enjoyable and accessible.

Ultimately, books and comics about black holes play a crucial role in educating young minds about the universe. They simplify complex theor es and spark interest in science, astronomy, and the mysteries of the cosmos.

As children read about black holes, they not only gain knowledge but also develop a sense of wonder about what lies beyond our planet, inspiring the next generation of astronomers and scientists to explore these supermassive mysteries.

How Popular Culture Shapes Our Understanding

Popular culture, including movies, books, and television shows, plays a significant role in shaping our understanding of complex scientific concepts like black holes. These fascinating cosmic phenomena capture our imagination, often depicted as mysterious and powerful forces. By featuring black holes in popular media, creators help introduce these concepts to younger audiences, making science more accessible and engaging. For example, movies like "Interstellar" explore themes of time travel and gravity, sparking curiosity about the universe's most enigmatic objects.

As I said earlier, when we watch a science fiction film that includes black holes, we often see them portrayed as swirling vortexes that can bend time and space. This dramatic representation captures the awe and wonder associated with these cosmic giants.

However, it's essential to remember that while these portrayals are entertaining, they are also rooted in real scientific theories. Theoretical models of black holes are based on Einstein's theory of relativity, which helps us understand how these massive objects influence their surroundings.

Moreover, popular culture allows us to explore the relationship between black holes and gravitational waves. These waves are ripples in space-time caused by massive cosmic events, such as the merging of black holes. By presenting these concepts in a fun and engaging way, movies and shows can inspire young audiences to learn more about the universe and the science behind it.

Understanding gravitational waves can be thrilling, especially when we see them represented in exciting narratives that make the science feel alive.

Black holes are not just fascinating on their own; they also play a crucial role in the broader context of cosmology. They help us understand how galaxies form and evolve over time. By incorporating black holes into stories, popular culture highlights their importance in shaping our universe. This connection makes it easier for children to grasp how these giant entities influence everything around them, including stars and planets.

Lastly, the idea of time travel often linked with black holes fuels our imagination and encourages critical thinking. Many stories suggest that traveling through a black hole could lead to different points in time or even alternate realities.

These theories, while currently speculative, inspire young minds to dream big and ask questions about the nature of time and space. Through engaging narratives, popular culture encourages curiosity about the universe, motivating the next generation of scientists to explore these supermassive mysteries.

Fascinating Fact

Some scientists think the very first black holes may have formed just moments after the Big Bang—long before stars or galaxies existed.

Chapter 5 – Key Takeaways

- Stellar black holes form after a supernova when a massive star collapses.

- Supermassive black holes may grow by swallowing matter or merging with others.

- Some black holes could have formed just after the Big Bang.

- Scientists are still figuring out exactly how the biggest black holes came to be.

6: The Role of Black Holes in Cosmology

Black Holes and the Evolution of the Universe

Black holes are some of the most mysterious objects in the universe. They are formed when massive stars run out of fuel and collapse under their own gravity. This collapse creates a region in space where the gravitational pull is so strong that nothing, not even light, can escape from it.

Because they are invisible, black holes can only be detected by observing their effects on nearby stars and gas. This makes them fascinating subjects for scientists and curious minds alike.

The evolution of the universe is deeply connected to the existence of black holes. As galaxies formed and evolved over billions of years, supermassive black holes began to appear at their centers. These giants can be millions or even billions of times more massive than our Sun!

Black holes have also captured the imagination of people in popular culture. They appear in movies, books, and even video games, often depicted as mysterious portals or gateways to other dimensions. This fascination helps spark interest in real science, as young people learn that black holes are not just science fiction, but very real phenomena that scientists are studying. By exploring black holes in stories, we can inspire future astronomers and physicists to uncover their secrets.

Gravitational waves are another exciting connection to black holes. When two black holes collide, they create ripples in space-time that travel outward at the speed of light. Do you remember that these waves were predicted by Albert Einstein over a century ago and were finally detected by scientists in 2015? This discovery opened up a new way of observing the universe and gave us a glimpse of the violent events that occur when black holes merge. Learning about gravitational waves helps us understand the dynamic processes that shape our cosmos.

Finally, black holes also raise intriguing questions about time travel and the nature of reality. Theoretical models suggest that if we could survive the intense gravity near a black hole, we might experience time differently. Some scientists theorize that traveling through a black hole could lead to another part of the universe or even a different time. While this idea sounds like science fiction, it encourages us to think about the possibilities of the universe and what lies beyond our current understanding.

Their Impact on Stars and Galaxies

Black holes are mysterious objects in space that have a huge impact on stars and galaxies. When a massive star runs out of fuel, it collapses under its own gravity and can become a black hole.

This process can create powerful explosions called supernovae, which scatter elements into space. These elements are essential for forming new stars and planets, showing that black holes play a crucial role in the life cycle of galaxies.

Supermassive black holes, which can be millions or even billions of times the mass of our sun, are found at the centers of many galaxies, including our Milky Way. They have a powerful gravitational pull that affects the orbits of nearby stars and gas. As material spirals into a black hole, it forms an accretion disk that heats up and emits intense radiation. This radiation can influence star formation in the surrounding areas, making black holes key players in shaping galaxies.

In addition to influencing the stars around them, black holes are also connected to the fabric of space and time. According to theoretical models, they can warp space-time, creating fascinating possibilities such as wormholes and even time travel.

These ideas have captured the imagination of many, leading to their portrayal in popular culture, from movies to books. This connection between science and storytelling makes black holes even more intriguing.

Another interesting aspect of black holes is their relationship with gravitational waves. Do you remember how when two black holes collide, they create ripples in space-time that travel across the universe? These gravitational waves can be detected by scientists on Earth, providing valuable information about black holes and their interactions. This discovery has opened up a new way of understanding the universe and the role black holes play in it.

Overall, black holes are not just cosmic vacuum cleaners; they are essential to the evolution of stars and galaxies. By studying them, scientists can learn more about the universe's history and its future. As we continue to explore these supermassive mysteries, we might uncover even more secrets about how black holes shape our cosmos.

Black Holes and Dark Matter

Black holes are one of the most fascinating and mysterious objects in the universe. They are formed when massive stars collapse under their own gravity at the end of their life cycle. The gravity of a black hole is so strong that nothing, not even light, can escape from it. This is why black holes are called 'black' - they do not emit light, making them invisible to the naked eye. Scientists use various methods to detect them, often observing the effects they have on nearby stars and gas clouds.

Dark matter is another mysterious component of our universe, and it plays a crucial role in the structure of galaxies. Unlike black holes, dark matter does not interact with light or any other form of electromagnetic radiation, making it invisible.

It is believed to make up about 27% of the universe, while ordinary matter, which includes stars and planets, only accounts for about 5%. The remaining 68% is thought to be dark energy, which is responsible for the accelerated expansion of the universe.

In popular culture, black holes have captured the imagination of many through movies, books, and video games. As I mentioned, films like Interstellar explore the concept of black holes and even depict time travel through them. These stories often blend science with fiction, allowing viewers to ponder the possibilities of traveling to distant places in space or different points in time. While these portrayals are exciting, they also spark interest in real scientific research about black holes and their effects on the universe.

Have you remembered this fact: Supermassive black holes, which can be millions or even billions of times the mass of our sun, are found at the centers of most galaxies, including our own Milky Way?

Their immense gravity influences the orbits of stars and gas in their vicinity, and they can even trigger the formation of new stars when material falls into them. Understanding supermassive black holes helps scientists unlock the mysteries of galaxy formation and the overall structure of the universe.

Black holes are also connected to the phenomenon of gravitational waves, ripples in spacetime created by massive objects like colliding black holes. When these waves pass through Earth, they can be detected by sensitive instruments, allowing scientists to study the universe in a new way. The study of black holes and gravitational waves not only deepens our understanding of the cosmos but also opens up exciting possibilities for theories about time travel and the nature of reality.

As we continue to explore these supermassive mysteries, we find ourselves asking even bigger questions about the universe and our place within it.

Fascinating Fact

When two black holes crash into each other, they release more energy in one moment than all the stars in the universe combined—for a few seconds!

Chapter 6 – Key Takeaways

- When black holes collide, they send out gravitational waves—ripples in space-time.

- LIGO and other observatories can detect these waves from Earth.

- Gravitational waves give us a new way to "see" black holes in action.

- These discoveries confirm predictions made by Einstein over a century ago.

7: Black Holes and Time Travel Theories

Can Black Holes Help Us Travel Through Time?

Have you ever wondered if black holes could help us travel through time? I have. In our universe, black holes are like giant cosmic vacuum cleaners, swallowing everything that comes too close. Some scientists believe that if we could somehow enter a black hole, we might find a way to jump into the past or future! This idea might sound like science fiction, but it comes from real theories in physics that explore how time and space are connected.

When we think about black holes, we often imagine them as mysterious and dangerous. However, they can also be fascinating! Black holes warp space around them so much that they can create paths called wormholes. These wormholes might act like shortcuts through space and time. If a spaceship could navigate one of these paths safely, it might just allow travelers to visit different eras in history or even see what the future holds.

In popular culture, black holes are often featured in movies and books, making them seem even more exciting. Stories, like "Interstellar", show characters traveling through black holes and experiencing time differently than we do on Earth.

These creative ideas spark our imaginations and get us thinking about how time travel could be possible. While these stories are fictional, they are inspired by real scientific concepts that researchers study today.

Black holes also play a crucial role in our understanding of the universe. They help scientists learn about how galaxies form and evolve. Supermassive black holes, which are found at the centers of galaxies, can influence the stars and planets around them. By studying these enormous cosmic giants, we gain insights into the very fabric of time and space, and how they interact with gravity.

While we may not be able to hop into a black hole and travel through time just yet, the mysteries they hold encourage us to keep asking questions. Scientists are continuously exploring these fascinating phenomena, pushing the boundaries of what we know. Who knows? One day, we might unlock the secrets of time travel, all thanks to the incredible power of black holes!

The Science Behind Time Travel Concepts

Time travel is a fascinating idea that has captured the imaginations of many, especially when we think about black holes. These mysterious cosmic giants are not just powerful vacuum cleaners of the universe; they also play a significant role in theories about how we might travel through time. Scientists believe that if we could harness the energy around a black hole, we might discover ways to bend the fabric of space and time itself.

One of the most exciting concepts in time travel involves the idea of wormholes. Think of a wormhole as a shortcut through space and time, like a tunnel connecting two distant points in the universe. Some scientists theorize that black holes could create these wormholes, allowing us to leap through time and space in ways we can only dream of. However, the reality of creating or finding a stable wormhole is still a big mystery.

In popular culture, black holes and time travel are often portrayed in movies and books, sparking curiosity among kids and adults alike. These stories sometimes exaggerate the possibilities, but they help us think about complex scientific ideas in a fun way. For instance, in movies like "Interstellar," which I've mentioned a few times because I love it! It's a really cool movie. In it, black holes are shown as gateways to different times, raising questions about what it would be like to experience time differently.

Gravitational waves, which are ripples in space-time created by massive objects like black holes, also play a crucial role in our understanding of the universe. As you now already know, when two black holes collide, they create waves that travel through space. Scientists can detect these waves and use them to learn more about how black holes work. This research gives us insights into the universe and could one day help us figure out how to travel through time.

In the end, the science behind time travel and black holes is still evolving. While we may not have the technology to travel through time just yet, the exploration of these cosmic wonders continues to inspire scientists and dreamers alike. Each new discovery brings us one step closer to unlocking the secrets of the universe, including the mysteries of time itself.

Popular Theories and Their Implications

Black holes are some of the most mysterious objects in the universe, and many theories exist to explain their nature and behavior. One popular theory is that black holes can form from the remnants of massive stars after they explode in supernovae.

This theory helps scientists understand how black holes come into existence and why they can vary in size, from stellar black holes to the supermassive ones found at the centers of galaxies. Each type has distinct characteristics, and this diversity adds to the excitement of studying these cosmic giants.

Another fascinating theory involves the idea of gravitational waves, which are ripples in space-time created by the acceleration of massive objects, like black holes. When two black holes collide, they produce strong gravitational waves that can be detected here on Earth.

This discovery has opened up a new way of observing the universe, allowing astronomers to learn more about black holes and the events that surround them. It's like listening to the universe play a symphony of cosmic events!

In popular culture, black holes have captured the imagination of many through movies, books, and games. They are often portrayed as mysterious gateways to other dimensions or time travel. For example, in the movie "Interstellar," black holes are depicted as portals that can transport astronauts to different parts of the universe. These imaginative stories inspire young minds to think about the possibilities of space travel and the adventures that await beyond our planet.

The role of black holes in cosmology is also significant. They help scientists understand the evolution of galaxies and the structure of the universe. Supermassive black holes, which can be millions to billions of times more massive than our sun, influence the formation of stars and the movement of galaxies. By studying them, researchers can uncover the secrets of how our universe came to be and how it continues to evolve over time.

Lastly, the theories surrounding black holes and time travel are particularly intriguing. Some scientists propose that if we could find a way to navigate a black hole, it might lead us to different points in time. While this idea remains theoretical and far from being proven, it captivates the imagination and encourages young explorers to dream big about the future of space travel. Who knows what mysteries we might uncover if we could unlock the secrets of black holes?

Fascinating Fact

Wormholes are based on real math, but no one has ever found one. If they do exist, they might collapse before anything could go through.

Chapter 7 – Key Takeaways

- Wormholes are theoretical shortcuts through space and time, but haven't been proven.

- Time travel is possible in theory, but not like in the movies.

- Space science and sci-fi often mix real ideas with wild imagination.

- Thinking about time, space, and travel near black holes stretches our minds.

8: The Future of Black Hole Research

New Discoveries on the Horizon

As we look to the stars, exciting new discoveries about black holes are on the horizon! Scientists are constantly working to better understand these mysterious giants that inhabit our universe. With advanced telescopes and new technology, we are getting closer to unveiling the secrets of supermassive black holes, which can weigh millions or even billions of times more than our sun. Each discovery brings us one step closer to answering questions about how these massive objects form and evolve over time.

One of the most thrilling aspects of modern astronomy is the study of gravitational waves. Remember, when two black holes collide, they create ripples in space-time that travel across the universe. These waves were first detected in...can you remember? It was 2015, and since then, scientists have been using them to learn more about black holes and their behaviors. Every new detection helps to confirm theories and offers a glimpse into the hidden dynamics of our cosmos.

In popular culture, black holes are often depicted as terrifying voids that consume everything in their path. Movies and books have sparked young imaginations with tales of space adventures and time travel. As science progresses, we are beginning to see how these fictional representations can inspire real scientific inquiry. Understanding black holes could lead to amazing possibilities, including theories about time travel and the very fabric of reality itself.

Moreover, researchers are exploring the role of black holes in shaping galaxies. Supermassive black holes are believed to be at the center of most galaxies, influencing their formation and evolution. This connection between black holes and galaxies is vital for understanding the universe's architecture. As we gather more data, we may uncover how these colossal entities interact with their surroundings and the stars they govern.

A famous scientist named Stephen Hawking came up with a surprising idea: black holes might not last forever. He believed that, over an incredibly long time, black holes could slowly lose energy and shrink. This idea is called *Hawking Radiation*. It means that even something as powerful and mysterious as a black hole might eventually fade away and vanish.

Scientists are still trying to understand how this works, but it's one of the most exciting ideas in modern space science.

Finally, the future of black hole research is bright. With upcoming missions and technological advancements, we are poised to make groundbreaking discoveries. Each piece of information adds to our cosmic puzzle, helping us understand not just black holes, but the universe as a whole. Stay tuned, because the next big breakthrough could be just around the corner!

The Tools and Technology Used in Research

In the quest to understand black holes, scientists rely on a range of advanced tools and technologies. Telescopes, for instance, are crucial for observing distant galaxies where these mysterious giants reside. High-powered telescopes can capture images of black holes and the surrounding matter, allowing researchers to study their behavior and properties even if they cannot be seen directly. This technology helps unlock the secrets of the universe, revealing the presence of supermassive black holes lurking at the centers of galaxies.

Another vital tool in black hole research is computer modeling. Scientists create theoretical models that simulate how black holes interact with their environment. These models help predict phenomena such as gravitational waves, which are ripples in spacetime caused by massive objects like colliding black holes.

Through simulations, researchers can test their ideas and refine their understanding of black holes, making it possible to explore concepts like time travel and the nature of the universe itself.

In addition to telescopes and computer models, scientists use satellites to gather data from space. Instruments aboard these satellites measure various cosmic phenomena, including radiation emitted by black holes. This information is crucial for understanding the energy output of black holes and how they influence their surroundings. As technology advances, the tools used in space research continue to evolve, providing new insights into the mysteries of our galaxy.

Gravitational wave detectors, such as LIGO, are groundbreaking technologies that have changed our understanding of black holes. These detectors can sense the incredibly small distortions in spacetime caused by events like black hole mergers. When two black holes collide, they emit gravitational waves that travel across the universe. By studying these waves, scientists can gather information about the masses and spins of the black holes involved, further enhancing our knowledge of their role in the cosmos.

Finally, the integration of artificial intelligence and machine learning is beginning to play a significant role in black hole research. These technologies can analyze vast amounts of data from telescopes and satellites much faster than humans. AI can help identify patterns and anomalies that might indicate the presence of a black hole or other cosmic phenomena. As we continue to explore the universe, these innovative tools and technologies will be essential in unraveling the supermassive mysteries that lie beyond our reach.

Encouraging Young Scientists to Explore the Cosmos

The cosmos is a vast and exciting place, filled with wonders that can spark the imagination of young minds. Encouraging young scientists to explore the mysteries of the universe, particularly black holes, can ignite a passion for science that lasts a lifetime. Black holes are not just the stuff of science fiction; they are real phenomena that play crucial roles in the structure of galaxies and the evolution of the universe. By understanding these cosmic giants, children can appreciate the complexity and beauty of the universe around them.

Young explorers can start their journey by learning about the different types of black holes, from the tiny primordial black holes to the supermassive black holes found at the centers of galaxies.

These entities have fascinating properties, like their ability to warp space and time, making them a perfect topic for curious minds. Engaging with theoretical models of black holes can help children visualize how these cosmic giants might behave and interact with other celestial bodies. This exploration not only enhances their knowledge but also fosters critical thinking and creativity.

Popular culture is another gateway for young scientists to engage with the concept of black holes. Movies, books, and video games often feature black holes and their mysterious nature, allowing children to see science in action.

By discussing these representations, kids can learn to differentiate between fact and fiction, sparking discussions about scientific accuracy and the real-life implications of black holes. This connection to popular culture makes learning about black holes exciting and relatable, encouraging them to delve deeper into the science behind these phenomena.

Also, black holes are intricately linked to groundbreaking concepts like gravitational waves and time travel theories. By introducing these ideas, educators can inspire children to think beyond traditional boundaries and explore cutting-edge scientific research. Understanding how black holes can produce gravitational waves opens up discussions about the fabric of space-time and the potential to unlock the secrets of the universe.

These concepts challenge young minds to dream big and consider careers in science, technology, engineering, and mathematics (STEM).

Ultimately, encouraging young scientists to explore the cosmos involves creating an environment where curiosity is celebrated. By providing resources, mentorship, and opportunities for hands-on experiences, we can empower the next generation to pursue their interest in black holes and cosmology. The universe is full of mysteries waiting to be uncovered, and with the right encouragement, today's youth can become the pioneers of tomorrow's astronomical discoveries.

Fascinating Fact

Tiny black holes might last longer than the whole universe—unless they're slowly losing energy. Even then, it would take longer than the universe has existed so far for one to disappear!

Chapter 8 – Key Takeaways

- Black holes may not live forever—they could shrink and slowly disappear over time.

- Scientists believe black holes lose tiny amounts of energy, bit by bit. This is called Hawking Radiation, named after famous physicist Stephen Hawking, who created the theory.

- This slow fading process would take billions or even trillions of years.

- Black holes might not be permarent parts of the universe after all.

Conclusion: So What Now?

Well, here we are—at the edge of the universe (okay, the back of the book), and you've just traveled through time, space, gravity, and mystery to get here. If your brain feels like it's had a workout... good! That means you've been thinking big—really big. Because black holes aren't just strange space stuff...they're proof that the universe is full of questions we *still* don't have answers to.

I've written about a lot of different things, and I have repeated a lot of ideas to help you remember—but this is a fun book, not a textbook, so it's not like you *have* to remember anything! You can always go back and read bits again. That's the great thing about books!

Some of the most brilliant scientists in history have spent their lives wondering about the same things you just read about. And guess what? There's still *so much* more to discover.

Maybe one day, you'll be the one building a telescope, running an experiment, or figuring out what's really inside a black hole. (And if you do, I want a signed photo, okay?)

So for now, stay curious. Keep asking those "But what if…?" questions. Whether you end up studying the stars or just stargazing for fun, you've taken a giant leap by learning about black holes. Who knows? Maybe one day, *you'll* be the one discovering something new

And whenever you look up at the night sky, just remember: you've already taken your first step into the universe.

Thanks for coming on this journey with me.

—Jake

📢 We'd Love to Hear What You Think!

If you or your family enjoyed *The Black Holes Book for Kids and Teens*, it would mean the world to us if you could leave a quick review on Amazon. Even just a sentence or two about what you liked helps other readers discover the book—and helps us keep making fun, educational books like this one!

👉 Important: Ideally, the Amazon account that purchased the book can leave a *verified purchase* review, so if a parent, grandparent, or teacher ordered it for you, ask if they'd be willing to post one on your behalf. If they can't, just go ahead and review it yourself!

Thank you for helping us spread the word—and for being the kind of reader who loves to learn! Here's QR you can scan to take you straight to the review page:

Or type this into your browser:

amazon.com/review/review-your-purchases/?asin=B0FC5T3PQL

Thanks!

Jake

The Black Holes Quiz!

SO: What have you learned from reading this book? Here's a fun quiz to test you, or you can use it to test friends and family, and see how much they really know about black holes—and then you can dazzle them with your encyclopedic knowledge!

The answers are listed afterwards—but no cheating, see how you get on first. I'm no expert on black holes and I wrote a book about them!

So it's okay if you get some wrong… I made the quiz star quite easy and get quite hard towards the end, to hopefully make it more fun for you.

1. What is a black hole?

2. Can light escape from a black hole?

3. What force is responsible for the creation of a black hole?

4. What is the invisible boundary around a black hole called?

5. What type of star collapses to form a stellar black hole?

6. Which is larger: a stellar black hole or a supermassive black hole?

7. What's the name of the glowing ring of gas and dust that spins around some black holes?

8. Where in our galaxy is the nearest supermassive black hole located?

9. What shape does the Milky Way galaxy have?

10. What effect causes time to slow down near a black hole?

11. What do scientists call the extreme stretching that happens if you fall into a black hole?

12. What tool helps scientists detect black holes through their effect on other stars?

13. What's one way scientists find black holes if they're invisible?

14. What happens when two black holes collide?

15. What do we call the ripples in space and time caused by black hole collisions?

16. What is LIGO used for?

17. What are wormholes believed to do—if they exist?

18. What's the difference between a black hole and a wormhole?

19. What theory did Albert Einstein create that helps explain black holes?

20. What's the name of the point inside a black hole where everything is crushed?

21. What does the word "accretion" mean in the context of black holes?

22. Why haven't scientists seen what's inside a black hole?

23. What does the idea of black holes fading away over time suggest about their future?

24. Why is Hawking radiation important in black hole science?

25. What is one question about black holes that scientists still don't know the answer to?

Black Holes Quiz Answer Key

Here's the **Answer Key** for the 25-question black hole quiz:

---

1. A black hole is a place in space with gravity so strong that nothing—not even light—can escape.

2. No, light cannot escape from a black hole.

3. Gravity.

4. The event horizon.

5. A massive star.

6. A supermassive black hole.

7. An accretion disk.

8. At the center of the Milky Way galaxy (Sagittarius A*).

9. A spiral shape.

10. Time dilation.

11. Spaghettification.

12. A telescope or by tracking the movement of nearby stars.

13. By observing how stars or gas move around it, or by detecting X-rays or gravitational waves.

14. They merge to form a larger black hole and release gravitational waves.

15. Gravitational waves.

16. To detect gravitational waves.

17. They are believed to connect two distant parts of space, like a shortcut.

18. A black hole pulls things in; a wormhole (in theory) connects two places.

19. The theory of relativity.

20. The singularity.

21. Material gathering or collecting around a black hole in a disk shape.

22. Because nothing, not even light, can escape to bring back information.

23. That black holes might not last forever—they could slowly shrink and disappear.

24. It suggests black holes lose energy over time, linking gravity with quantum physics.

25. Answers may vary: for example, "What happens inside a black hole?" or "How exactly do supermassive black holes form?"

📖 Glossary

A glossary is a special list of important words from the book, along with what they mean—kind of like a mini-dictionary just for black hole terms!

Accretion Disk
A hot, spinning ring of gas and dust swirling around a black hole. It glows so brightly that it helps scientists find where black holes are hiding.

Astrophysics
The science of space stuff—how stars, black holes, and galaxies work using the rules of physics.

Black Hole
A place in space with gravity so strong that nothing—not even light—can escape. Super cool. Super scary. Super real.

Cosmology
The science of how the universe began, what it's made of, and how it changes over time.

Dark Matter
A type of invisible stuff that makes up most of the universe. We can't see it, but we know it's there because of the way it moves things around.

Event Horizon

The invisible edge of a black hole. Cross it, and you're not coming back. Not even light can escape!

Galaxy

A giant collection of stars, planets, gas, dust—and usually a black hole or two! Our galaxy is called the Milky Way.

Gravitational Waves

Ripples in the fabric of space-time caused by huge events like black holes crashing together. Scientists can now *hear* them using special detectors.

Hawking Radiation

A theory that says black holes might slowly leak energy over time and eventually disappear. Named after the famous scientist Stephen Hawking.

Intermediate Black Hole

A medium-sized black hole—bigger than a stellar one but smaller than a supermassive one. Still pretty mysterious!

Light-Year

The distance that light travels in one year—nearly 6 trillion miles! Astronomers use it to measure really big space distances.

LIGO

A high-tech observatory that listens for gravitational

waves from things like black hole collisions. Kind of like a giant space ear.

Milky Way

Our home galaxy! A huge spiral of stars (including our Sun), planets, and cosmic stuff—with a supermassive black hole in the middle.

Neutron Star

What's left behind when a huge star explodes. It's super tiny, super heavy, and almost became a black hole.

Singularity

The center of a black hole where all its mass gets squished into an unbelievably tiny point. A place where physics gets weird.

Spaghettification

A real science word! It means being stretched out like spaghetti if you fall into a black hole. Not recommended.

Stellar Black Hole

A black hole made from a single star that ran out of fuel and collapsed. They're the most common kind.

Supermassive Black Hole

A black hole that's *millions or billions* of times heavier than the Sun! Usually found in the center of galaxies.

Theory of Relativity

Albert Einstein's famous theory explaining how space, time, and gravity all work together. It's a big deal in black hole science.

Time Dilation

Time moves slower near something with huge gravity—like a black hole. So someone near a black hole might age differently than someone far away!

Wormhole

A theoretical tunnel that could connect two faraway places in space (or time!). We haven't found one yet—but it makes awesome sci-fi.

Made in United States
Cleveland, OH
11 July 2025

18473463R00056

The
Black Holes
Book
for Kids and Teens

by
Jake Landon

BLENDON
PUBLISHING

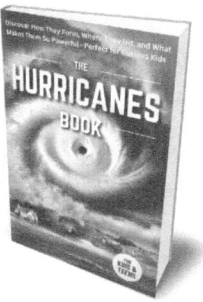

Also by JAKE LANDON from Blendon Publishing

THE **EXTREME ANIMALS SERIES**

Book 1 available now!

The Sharks Book for Kids & Teens

Discover the World's Fiercest Predators,
How They Survive, and Why They Matter —
Perfect for Curious Kids Who Love Wild Animals!

Coming soon — Snakes, Big Cats, Deadly Creatures and more!

AVAILABLE NOW ON AMAZON

For Hannah

Chapters